DON'T LET

Jody

STEAL

YOUR

Relationship

Common Sense For Uncommon Times

R FIELD TAYLOR

authorHOUSE

AuthorHouse™
1663 Liberty Drive
Bloomington, IN 47403
www.authorhouse.com
Phone: 833-262-8899

Published by AuthorHouse 09/23/2021

ISBN: 978-1-6655-3775-9 (sc)
ISBN: 978-1-6655-3776-6 (e)

Library of Congress Control Number: 2021918660

Print information available on the last page.

This book is dedicated to my wife Lynne who has always been my inspiration and managed to love me even at times when I could not love myself.

Don't Let Jody Steal Your Relationship

❖ ⟫⟫⟫⟫⟫⟫⟫⟫⟫⟫⟫⟫⟫⟫⟫⟫⟫⟫⟫⟫ ⟨♡⟩ ⟪⟪⟪⟪⟪⟪⟪⟪⟪⟪⟪⟪⟪⟪⟪⟪⟪⟪⟪⟪⟪ ❖

*T*oday I see a lot of people spending a lot of money on counseling sessions hoping to find some secret recipe which will change their potted meat and crackers marriage into a five-course sizzling steak buffet. In reality the only real objective they're achieving is making some rich person with a college degree even richer.

To understand the total concept of marriage we first have to take a trip back in time to human evolution when homosapiens didn't give a damn about being committed to a specific member of the opposite sex. To early man the more women he slept with increased the chances of producing more offspring which in turn would contribute to the survival rate of the entire group by creating more gatherers, hunters, and protectors. The women not only shared the communal responsibilities of child rearing but they also knew they were sharing their men as well. This system worked well from a biological standpoint. Nobody was singing "keep it on the down low" or "I left home to be with my sidepiece".

Then came the creation of different religions and the concept of one Adam for one Eve. These types of various beliefs in different mythologies which ranged from talking animals and plants to entire cities which existed above the clouds governed by some old guy sitting in a chair while holding a lightning bolt. These beliefs provided an early road map to creating norms and values in which we still practice in our everyday societies.

Before our societies evolved people viewed marriage as a right of achievement for any God fearing man or woman. A woman who was past 30 years old and still unmarried was considered an old maid and frowned upon and even worse was said of a man who chose not to wed and give offspring. Sometimes even the marriage itself was arranged in order to "keep good stock".

In some cases there were even what was known as "shotgun" weddings where if a young man impregnated a young woman their vows were said supported by the threat of the father of the bride and his shotgun.

Fast forward to this millennium and we see marriages derived from a variety of venues such as political, economical, religious, or even social entertainment. Everything depends on what qualities are being sought after in the nuptial agreements. Here in North Carolina a man may look for a woman who is skilled at changing the oil in a car while a woman may look for a man whose favorite meal is beanies and weenies straight from the can. Either way here are a few suggestions for men and women seeking to get the most residual happiness from their marriage investment.

Men

1) Help your wife to grow and evolve into the type of woman that pleases you. Whenever she does something to your liking, always show gratefulness and appreciation. If she cooks dinner and fixes your plate while bringing it to you don't say things like "you forgot the hot sauce". Remember Jody is always waiting to let your wife know how much she means to him.

2) Stop bringing all of these men into your home and introducing them to your wife. It's okay to be a good host but make sure you don't offer your wife as an appetizer to one of your thirsty friends just waiting on you to slip. Remember Jody doesn't have to sneak through your bedroom window if you're the one opening the front door for him.

3) Never compliment another woman's beauty in the presence of your wife. The only exception is if the target woman is over 75 years and still it should be done sparingly. If she wakes up in the morning all clad in

hair rollers, holey drawers, and slobber trails emerging from the corners of her mouth your first words should be "good morning baby, how do you always wake up looking so beautiful". Complimenting a woman is like making sure your foundation is level before building your house. If you're off three inches at the bottom you'll be off three feet at the top. Remember how you start determines how you finish.

4) Always be a provider. Never come home empty handed. If you unfortunately reach a place of unemployment as to no fault of your own you should continue to perform your manly duties leaving the house early in the morning seeking work and not returning until later in the evening with at least something to show for your efforts. Nothing ends a marriage quicker than for a woman to get up and go to work leaving a husband to sit home all day playing video games and finishing off an entire box of Cornflakes.

5) Fix your backbone. If it's one thing a good wife can do without, it's a wimpy husband. Sometimes no matter how independent a woman may go out of her way to appear secure, nothing makes her feel more secure at times than when her husband says "sit your ass down – you ain't going nowhere". While it's customary to include your spouse in all of the important decision making criteria your first response even to your friends should not be "let me ask my wife". Any man a woman can set her clock by is seen as far too predictable and nobody appreciates a predictable man more than Jody.

Women

1) Always be afraid of spiders and roaches. A man wants to be seen as a knight in shining armor protecting his wife from all threats real and imagined so a little theatrical work will do wonders for your husband's ego. Even though we all know you can make your size 10 high heel sing a song in somebody's ass sometimes you need to learn the fine art of falling back. At the sight of anything even remotely frightening, seek your husband's assistance and if you weigh less than 120 pounds you can even jump into his arms while screaming "save me, save me!"

2) Let your good housekeeping speak for itself. They say the way to a man's heart is through his stomach but in truth no man is putting anything in his mouth that comes from a dirty kitchen. When a man comes from work the first thing to excite his senses should be the smell of spring flowers radiating from the Febreeze wall plug-in. There should be no clutter in the living area or kitchen. Some women will be quick to state "it is

his responsibility too" but in all actuality most men are allowed a pass in this category. A woman's home is the flagship example of her wifely status especially to her girlfriends who may visit from time to time. If a wife is truly consistent in keeping a clean home it will inadvertently sow seeds in her husband's behavior to follow suit.

3) Don't compare your husband to another man especially an ex-lover. There is an old saying that words said in anger are like wounds that heal but still leave scars. A wife's objective should always be to build her husband up not tear him down. Just because Jody is keeping your girlfriend's car washed and waxed along with her grass kept neatly cut don't foolishly assume that stating a comparison between your husband and Jody will inspire your husband to suddenly start sleeping with a lawnmower in the middle of the bed. More than likely it will create issues of resentment and create suspicions.

4) Initiate sex at unpredictable times. Men are turned on by women who want to take them to bed. In your grandmother's day it would have seemed unladylike to pursue your husband for sexual favors while maintaining a passive approach to being satisfied within a marriage but today's norms are so much more advanced. An intelligent wife knows how to possess and utilize the power between her legs in ways to cause her modest husband suffering from self esteem issues to be able to stand in front of a mirror and see the reflection of a

superhero (cape included). Simply put the "knowing" wife will use what she's got to get what she wants.

5) Practice deferred gratification. Don't be ashamed of a husband who is driving a Ford Focus to work in order to save up to buy you a Mercedes. Too many wives get caught up in the present and never realize their husband's future potential. Marriage vows seldom come with instant fame and wealth unless you're marrying a prince from Saudi Arabia. It takes years for any relationship to blossom into its full potential. The flower depends on the rain as much as it does the sun because it knows how to be patient. Don't throw away tomorrow's dollar chasing today's dime.

Couples

1) Don't let nobody take care of your business better than you do. When a married couple shares information about how much money they have in the bank, how far behind they are on bills, how their spouse isn't pleasing them in bed or even what the doctor said they are unknowingly allowing others to give input and indirectly make decisions for the married couple. While a husband may occasionally have an argument with his wife he has very little chance of surviving arguments with all of his in-laws, mainly his wife's mother. When someone who doesn't even live with you can tell you how many cookies are in your cookie jar you have a leak in your house somewhere.

2) Learn to communicate without using words. Sometimes silence can pierce as loud as a scream. A lack of eye contact, going to bed early alone, a loose hand hold, and an over interest in the television can all be forms of silent communication. A skilled spouse will take time to learn this hidden art of communication without the

need of being verbally prodded along. In one example, sometimes a man will think he's getting away with deception due to his wife's lack of verbal reprimands but in reality it's her silence he should fear most of all. When she stops asking where you've been you know it's time to bring it on in.

3) Clean up what you mess up. To think that no one will ever make a mistake can be dismissed everytime you look at the eraser on top of a pencil. Throughout a marriage both parties will at some point do something so stupid it defies all logic but what determines the stability of the union is how the two parties get beyond the wreckage. If a person admits they made a mistake and attempt to try to fix it then the other party should not be so high and mighty that they can't show forgiveness. What goes around comes around, and if all a person looks for in a marriage is for the other to make a mistake then it's almost guaranteed that sooner or later they'll find what they're looking for. A simple rule of thumb is take turns forgiving each other.

4) If B.B. King tells you "The thrill is gone" you need to tell him he's a damn lie because you stay ready to go from the window to the wall. A marriage has got to be spontaneous in a large majority of occurrences ranging from unplanned get aways to surprise kisses behind the ear unannounced. If you do something different everyday you'll never grow old. Be able to vividly recall the first moment you knew you were in love and do whatever it takes to keep that feeling alive. This is what

it means to truly marry your soulmate. Everytime you send flowers to her job for no special reason makes Jody so mad he could pull all of his hair out.

5) Best friends stay married forever. Husbands and wives divorce every day. You have to know the person you walked down the aisle with, not just the person who makes you happy when they buy you a gift or give you sex. You should be able to share your innermost secrets about anything without fear of the information being used against you later. Real friends take turns crying in each other's arms while protecting each other from all the pain the world has to give and sometimes even from each other if need be. Sometimes throughout a marriage the storms of life can severe the bonds of husband and wife but never can a union of two best friends be easily broken. Where two are joined - one cannot easily fall without the other.

Everybody Kneeling Ain't Praying

*T*here was once a time when a man could pick any woman off the street, put a ring on her finger and send her to church three times a week and she would halfway do right but as I mentioned earlier this is a different day and age. Today if the preacher walks up to your wife holding a Bible while dropping to one knee, to the rest of the congregation it may look like he's praying but in reality he is trying to see what's under her dress.

Church folk are getting divorced at a higher rate than the old married couples who drink and cuss each other out everyday. Trying to keep a vow of loyalty based on a system of divinity which can't be seen or proven is like telling a religious fox not to eat any hens because they are holy. It is only when we accept the fact that human beings are creatures of habit designed to be biologically predisposed to seek pleasure and avoid pain that we understand that all of the Sunday School in the world can't save a marriage not built on a spiritual platform where two individuals honor each other as if they were God's in their own right.

Too Good To Ride In a Cadillac

ometimes we can be in so much of a rush to put a ring on someone's finger that we choose to overlook obvious tell tell signs that would have made us pump our brakes. In a rush to consummate matrimony we become blind to the fact that sometimes we are purchasing damaged goods.

If your new centerfold looking significant other just recently came away from two previous relationships where both her ex husbands drove cadillacs then how long do you think she will continue to ride in the front seat of your Ford with the doughnut on the back? Even though everyone has the ability to change, sometimes some of us can't see due to looking so hard.

Ain't Nobody Stole Your Man

How many times have we heard some wife making angry assertions that some slut stole her man? By theory the same slut carjacked the husband at gunpoint forced him to go to the nearest motel and tortured him until he unwillingly provided her with hours of reluctant sex. This scenario would have been more accepted than claiming someone 'stole her man'.

The question at hand is how can someone steal something which was offered or given away? When did all of this happen?

When the wife stopped coming to bed in a sexy bra and panties and was fast asleep within minutes. When the wife stopped calling on his lunch break just to let him know she was thinking about him. When she stopped caring about how she looked in public hair unfixed with clothes full of wrinkles. When she would meet him at the door engaging in a new argument everyday before he even had time to remove his work boots.

The truth is that many women through actions of their own unknowingly offer their men away into the arms of another. The great singer Laura Lee once said "If you can beat me rocking you can have my chair".

He Say She Say

ow many times have people in marriage relationships come to conclusions based on evidence of nothing more than the careless whispers of an envious friend or resentful enemy? People outside of the marriage are quick to advise one or even both of the partners that they should leave the other, even going as far to say that if they themselves were in that position they would have been left a long time ago. The one piece of vital information these outsiders fail to offer is why they remain single and unattached.

It has been stated on numerous occasions that misery loves company. It is without coincidence that old people advise newlywed couples to interact with others who are also married because when times of trouble occur within the marriage it will be a benefit to hear suggestions on how to save the marriage as opposed to finding ways to dissolve it. If you want a successful and happy marriage you should feed single people from a long handle spoon.

Play Your Position

$\mathcal{A}$ football team could never hope to win anything close to a championship unless every player on the field knew what specific responsibilities were expected of them. If a 300 pound guard was required to rush downfield to catch a pass thrown by a second string field goal kicker while being blocked for by a 90 pound tight end the results would be nothing less than total failure.

For a marriage to work efficiently both husband and wife must be willing to fulfill each of their respective responsibilities. This involves using assessments which were obtained throughout the dating years. Who had the better financial discipline, who had the least amount of procrastination, who was more inclined to "go the hell off". It is a known fact that a house divided cannot stand and no matter how much those forward thinking egalitarians might have you thinking that it's okay for a husband to spend three hours getting his hair done while being given a manicure the laws of nature never intended for a husband to compete with his wife to see who can look the most pretty. By the same comparison it was never intended for a married woman to work multiple jobs in order to compete with husband for the breadwinner status. Since it is a biological fact that most males are larger and stronger than females, nature has given us a hint on whose job it is to be the provider and protector while nature provided women the unique ability to conceive, birth, and nurture a newborn human being. Women also have an area of their brain better equipped for reasoning and emotional response.

Consider for an instance a giant earth moving bulldozer able to move tons of dirt equivalent to the work of hundreds of men. While this machinery is an asset in itself it also requires an operator able to perform maneuvers, read gauges, and not run over the dumb ass who is talking on a cellphone oblivious to the giant machine approaching him from behind. Assume for a moment that the machine and operator traded places leaving the operator to manually shovel thousands of tons of dirt while the machine sat unattended devoid of any cognitive thought of action.

The result would be hardly any work being completed. Marriage works in the same way for husbands and wives. Not only should each one know their position but also be knowledgeable to fulfill it with proficiency.

There is an old saying "You'll never strike gold working in a silver mine". Playing your position is vital to a happy marriage.

Nobody Knows Where The Nose Goes When The Doors Are Closed

———— ❦ ————

A husband and wife should be willing to do whatever is required of them within the confines of their bedroom. There should be no such thing as taboo or out of bounds for a married couple. Anything less than 100 percent commitment is equal to leaving the door open for Jody (and Jody can be a woman sometimes also).

Decades ago things such as oral sex, role playing and watching porn were things no self respecting husband or wife would ever totally agree to participating in but now a man who refuses to engage in oral sex every now and then will lose his woman faster than a set of car keys.

The role for a good wife has always been to be a lady in the streets and a freak in the bedroom. Ladies would be surprised at what a little vocal coaching in the bedroom could do for their marriage. In other words, "Holla!" even if he isn't in the right spot. Intelligent women know this is where you mold your man into the husband you want him to be. The whole time he thinks he is "standing up in it" the woman is turning a zero into a hero. Honesty is one of the most valuable assets in a marriage agreement to sustain longevity but the bedroom is the only place where "Fake it till you make it" can be used as a mission statement.

Don't Think They Aint Watching

---

*J*ust because you attempt to keep most of your marriage life away from scrutiny and the public eye sometimes you can inadvertently let the whole world know what's going on inside your home just by the way your significant other carries themselves. When a woman drives around in a dirty car with the gas light on - it's a man somewhere that aint doing their job. When a woman leaves the house with tracks showing and run over heels on her shoes - it's a man somewhere that aint doing his job. When a woman has to borrow money to get her Time Warner Cable cut back on - it's a man somewhere that aint doing his job.

By the same token when you see a man who's entire wardrobe came from Walmart- there's a woman somewhere who aint doing her job. When you see a man who only has bologna sandwiches everyday for lunch on a 12 hour shift- there's a woman somewhere that aint doing her job. When a man invites his friend over but can't offer him anything to drink because there are no clean cups - it's a woman somewhere who aint doing her job.

While we think small things like this go unnoticed all of the "Jodys" pay close attention to every detail. This is why a young husband could lose his wife to a full tank of gas or a young wife lose her husband to a plate of fried chicken and potato salad.

Feed Em Till They Look Like You

So many marriages today involve children from former relationships. Being a good step parent is just as important as being a good husband or wife. Old people's wisdom still decides that if you marry a woman with children then you should treat those children as your own.

It has been said that a lot of men would show signs of great insecurity when the step children are an everyday face of the new wife's ex husband or boyfriend. This usually resulted in the children being mistreated and the marriage being terminated. The remedy for this situation if two people genuinely love each other is to feed those kids until they start to look like you.

A good husband and stepfather will almost always pass on traits to his stepchildren even without a biological connection. The mature outlook of a husband and wife will mutually acknowledge that the children had no responsibility in the arrangement of two adults consenting vows to each other. At no point should a wife place her marriage requirements above the needs of her children. A good husband will attend to the needs of his step children sometimes even before the needs of his wife. This simple act alone separates the definition of a "boyfriend" and a "husband".

In the event that someone fails to step up and honor their responsibilities, Jody is always available to take the children shopping, to the park, and if given enough notice will even show up to football practices and school plays.

Jody Loves Birdwatching

*I*f it's one type of bird Jody loves more than any other,
it's a jailbird. Jody will rise early in the morning to read
the local newspaper, search the internet for new mugshots,

even taking rides throughout the neighborhood noticing certain cars in the driveway which have shown no signs of being driven lately.

Throughout some marriages some couples may be forced to experience the unwanted dilemma of incarceration. This situation could prove to be fatal for young marriages still in their infancies. The vows which were taken really come to light as many wives are forced to readjust their lives without the presence of a significant other. Most of the time a wife's faithfulness will be a direct correlation as to the length of the imposed jail/prison sentence. In the beginning both parties focus on dedication, trust, and loyalty but after a few missed visits and zero balances on payphone accounts the old cold hand of reality slowly puts the marriage relationship in a stranglehold. A few strong women have been known to wait patiently for years while for many Jody is placing his suits in the closet in less than 30 days.

Jody's new responsibilities include making sure the husband has money on his canteen account, driving the wife to visitation at least once a month, and introducing himself to all the neighbors as the new live in cousin from out of town.

There will be many nights when the incarcerated husband using the inmate payphone will ask his wife "who is that I hear in the background?" to which she will only respond "it's only the T.V.".

The only sure way to avoid this situation is for a new husband to abstain from any lifestyle which could result in being locked up indefinitely leaving your wife and children in the care of Mr. Jody.

Sometimes We Can't See For Looking

$\mathcal{A}$ person would think that Jody would always be the slim attractive young man with the six pack abs or the young woman with the long hair and coke bottle shape but in reality they could be no farther from the truth. Jody is the old widow woman driving the new Cadillac looking for someone to clean her car. Jody is the old man with the bald spot and protruding belly fat offering to pay a young lady's cell phone bill. Jody is the fat girl everyone secretly calls "Precious". Jody is Reverend Trueblood known to make house calls and lay hands on people. Jody is the Food Lion cashier that helped bag you and your spouse's grocery. Jody is your second cousin on your daddy's side. Jody is the guy who doesn't own a car or license but drives your car more than you do. Jody is your Aunt Mary who keeps dropping off sweet potato pies while you're at work. Jody was your husband's best man at your wedding. Jody was the girl who came up to the car asking for spare change. Jody was the guy laying in the casket you said was a friend of your brothers.

Jody is the old man in a wheelchair in the nursing home who paid your way through college. Jody is the preacher's wife when he does an out of town sermon. Finally, Jody is the one who goes fishing everyday using bait so good it can't even be purchased in a store.

As we navigate our way through the rocky cliffs and hidden valleys of marriage we are reminded of a biblical quote which shall summarize our entire agenda.

(What God has joined together, let no man put asunder).

Give A Person Time To Miss You

When Barry White said "too much of a good thing aint good for you" he must have known somewhere there would be a married couple who woke up with each other, went to work with each other, rode home with each other, and watched television before going to bed with each other.

The quickest way to put a fire out is to smother it. The whole purpose of a bride and groom not being able to see each other the entire day before the wedding was to build up excitement for each other on their honeymoon night. Even though you may love someone until death do you part doesn't mean you won't get tired of smelling their breath in your face every time you turn around to make a move.

Learning to feel secure in a relationship without constant validation is a must if any type of growth is to be expected. Even though attachment issues first make an appearance in people's infancies when a mother briefly leaves a room out of eyesight from a newborn who interprets her temporary absence as total abandonment they sometimes carry over into adulthood in the disguise of arrested development where one person's quick trip to the convenience store can be read as an attempt to end the relationship.

No matter how much closeness is shared within the marriage there should always be some form of self identity withheld to ensure a person's confidence and individuality. It was some greek philosopher who made the statement "absence makes the heart grow fonder".

The way Jody uses this to his advantage is he never allows a person to enjoy his company on an everyday basis. He intentionally lets the majority of phone calls go to voicemail and once in a while he will even purposely call off a planned date due to some unforeseen emergency. While all of this may seem like destructive social skills Jody knows these acts will also create a more unquenchable desire.

The main benefit of creating a small amount of space is that a person finally gets to find out who they are as opposed to just being a good husband or a good wife. If a marriage can not withstand small periods of separation without collapsing or imploding within itself then it was never really formulated on solid values such as trust and honesty.

In the old days a husband could leave the house, stand in the front yard while waving to his wife and say "Honey I'll return home before the grass grows back". To which she would lovingly respond "If you aint back before dark, stay your ass where you at". This would be the tell tell signs of a happy and fruitful marriage.

If You Aint Got No Money Stay Your Broke Ass Home

Nothing can be worse than for a husband and wife to sit at the restaurant table alongside other married couples and pretend to look content with only ordering from the appetizer menu. This isn't so bad until you ask for two plates in order to split and share one loaded potato while explaining to the group how you just ate before leaving the house. You then spend the rest of the evening looking at half eaten meals of shrimp and filet mignon as the waiter removes dishes from the table while your stomach continues to rumble. Inside you just want to stand up and say "If y'all aint going to eat that…"

One thing that will send any marriage into a quick financial nose dive is the tendency to splurge constantly on unnecessary items.

While it is the highlight of any romantic evening to finish with a candle light dinner complete with a sweet french red wine, the compulsion to expect this type of dining every night would prove to be a drain on the newly wedded bank account. Your mother-in-law bought you a microwave as a wedding gift for good reason.

Food, drinks, and social entertainment can soon turn assets into liabilities. As we've mentioned in the previous chapter the art of falling back is a financial must at times.

A married couple should be able to find love and happiness at home without the expensive price tag of acquiring more debt. There should be no shame in having to decline an invitation if it means not struggling at the end of the week to pay a utility bill. If the Jones' next door purchase a new car your reaction should be "congratulations" not making a trip down to the dealership. No matter how much effort a couple puts in they will never be able to keep up with Mr. and Mrs. Jones.

When couples allow themselves to become financially over extended in the marriage, Jody finds it all too convenient to come by and lend a helping hand. His trademark slogan is "Just let me know if you need something". He will gladly offer a little help until you see brighter days and will work out some creative method for you to pay back the debt or "work it off".

The lesson to be learned is don't try to live above your means and be content with entertaining each other at home at times. So when the couple next door tries to entice you with purchasing cars, vacations, and shopping sprees in which you are certain you can't afford, your ending response should be "aint nothing going on but the rent".

When A Rabbit Has More Than One Hole

$\mathcal{I}$t has been shown many times that a good hound can be outsmarted by a clever rabbit avoiding capture by retreating to a hidden hole oblivious to the hound. Just because the hound observed the rabbit exiting a certain location he mistakenly assumed that was the rabbit's only hole and instead of following the rabbit he chose to abort the chase and guard the only hole known to him. Needless to say the rabbit ended up stretching out relaxed in his alternate hole with his middle finger extended.

Just because we place rings on our significant other's finger does not make the multitude of ex lovers simply vanish into thin air. A good spouse will take time to learn as much as possible about all of these past acquaintances even down to which ones are still accepting applications. Keep your friends close and your enemies closer.

Becoming knowledgeable does not mean there is a hint of distrust in the air, it only means that you're doing extra credit work in order to secure your lifetime investment.

There have been many occasions when Jody will browse through the pages of a high school yearbook looking to reignite the fires of an old flame. The concept of someone being currently married will have little or no effect on him initiating a reunion for old times sake. His war cry will be "I was with them before they got married".

The best defense against Jody coming back through time and snatching your husband or wife is to familiarize yourself with his name, looks, city of residence, and even what type of car he drives. This will not allow Jody to be able to hide in plain sight. Jody will never announce who he is if you fail to recognize him first neither will your husband or wife be too quick to bring it to your attention. Sometimes there is no substitute for doing good homework.

In the event your spouse may have had numerous attractions in their past don't allow yourself to become consumed with focusing on only one. Remember it's usually the bus you don't see that ends up running over you.

When You Can't Kill Nothing And Nothing Won't Die

*T*here will come a time when you feel as though you've endured all you can take and did the best you can and you still end up losing at no fault of your own. Your luck will be so bad that it seems as though you can shoot in the air and kill a fish.

There is a lot of truth to the old saying - good guys finish last - because if you are not willing to get down and dirty to play the same game Jody is playing he knows he will always have you at a disadvantage. In your heart of hearts you know that you are a loving and devoted spouse who has given out the I forgive you card on numerous occasions yet somehow you still end up on the losing end. Rather than continue to fight a losing battle and walk away with nothing in this rare instance you should raise the white flag and offer a truce.

You should let Jody know that from this point forward the house payment will be divided three ways, the car note will be divided three ways, and everyone will be responsible for their own food.

Inform Jody of his designated day to drop the kids off at school and take the dog to the vet. The closet space should be rearranged to accommodate belongings for three as well as the queen size bed upgraded to king.

You should have weekly business meetings in where you go over financial statements and strategies informing Jody that you don't plan on going anywhere until you recoup one hundred and fifty percent of your marriage investment including the 39 dollar ab machine you purchased from Walmart with a gift card.

In no way do you allow Jody to profit from someone misleading you or using your kindness against you. The tears you withhold in resentment will soon turn into tears of joy. After collecting all of your compensation for years of being faithfully married, the last item you should place on the kitchen table as you walk out the door should be the 4.99 receipt for the five pound bag of Dixie Crystal sugar you unselfishly shared between the two of their gas tanks.

Teach Me How To Dougie

One of the single most reasons married couples drift apart from each other is simply because one person out grows the other. Any marriage which becomes stagnated and allows itself to fall into the soft cushions of complacency is only a ticking time bomb for Jody to make an appearance.

While one member of the married team religiously watches adventurous television shows such as the travel channel always looking for the next great road trip while the other only looks forward to a Friday night pizza delivery, this will eventually cause noticeable tension and repressed anxiety which will almost always present itself in the form of an argument seeming to emerge from out of thin air.

This is why it is almost imperative that couples find an unending amount of hobbies, interests, and projects which allow them to grow their experiences together creating new mutual bonds. Husbands and wives should be able to identify and measure different types of growth throughout the duration of the marriage.

There have been occasions where a newly wed couple

would be in attendance of some dance where when the song "electric slide" was played one of them would have to voluntarily sit out due to not being able to perform the front, back, and side to side routine. The good spouse would make it their mission to learn these particular sequences even if it resulted in being seen as the only one on the dance floor with two left feet. The failing spouse would simply admit to not knowing and make no attempt to learn.

Many open doors have been left for Jody to make his entrance due to a spouse's refusal to participate in couple related activities or discussions. Jody makes it a priority to stay well read on a host of different topics even being able to recite the current best selling novel. Jody is always the one who is never afraid to go into the water at the beach. Jody always orders something from the menu which requires a slight accent to pronounce. The most important attribute which Jody keeps readily available within his arsenal of weapons of infidelity is his uncanny ability to keep from becoming stereotyped. This means you may find him rock climbing, jet skiing, or even skydiving.

Synchronicity is defined as two individual units moving in unison with each other. This unison doesn't have to be identical but it does have to exhibit equal initiatives. One person's goal to obtain a higher level of education could be paralleled by a spouse learning to perform at home automobile mechanics. Both interests while being separate and unique still share the common denominator of growth.

The same way computers require constant updates, spouses' must constantly upgrade their marriage software. What someone knew ten years ago will not be compatible with their spouse's current update on marital happiness. The primary objective is to remain relevant.

For the spouse who chooses to stay home while the other makes their weekly gym appointment - have no worries, Jody is standing at the entrance with a towel in hand waiting to assist. Remember - a marriage ends when growth dies.

Stop Hustling Backwards

*I*n any given relationship the sum is supposed to equal greater than either of the individual partners alone.

In one example a young lady with fairly decent credit making an above average income was ecstatic when she was finally able to say her marriage vows including the parts relating to sickness and health along with richer or poorer.

In less than a year she saw her credit begin to decline due to excessive cash advances which were used to pay a constantly delinquent mortgage. Where there had been two cars in the driveway there now resided only one with the other in need of various mechanical repairs. On chilly mornings she would find herself having to rely on the warmth of the heat generated from the kitchen oven because the natural gas company failed to deliver due to non-payment.

Along with all of the living inconveniences came the constant arguments of how money was spent. Everyday of the once fairytale presumed marriage was actually a manifestation of hell. The nuptial agreements no longer seemed important since there was rarely any opportunity to find happiness. Every suggestive hint at restructuring their finances was interpreted as a subliminal attack against manlihood.

One day in desperation she chose to confide her dilemma to a male coworker during one of the thirty minute lunch breaks taken in the company break room. While noticing tears beginning to form in corners of her eyes he gently reached out taking hold of her hand while using the phrase so readily memorized by all members of the Jody clan, "Honey you can do bad by yourself - you don't need a man to help you with that".

The one thing that will save a marriage from entering the gates of divorce court is the ability to distinguish a temporary slump from a fatal crash and burn. If two people come together with only a nickel each in their pocket then by the end of the first year of marriage they should at least have been able to accumulate a total of three nickels between the two of them.

Sometimes it's easier for someone to pull you down instead of you pulling them up. Having faith and knowing that a significant other will do whatever it takes to go the extra mile is crucial to sustaining a prosperous marriage. Rule number one is choosing someone who doesn't have the same vices or "bad habits" as yourself.

If you smoke, drink, and like to party on the weekends then it would be borderline stupidity to seek out a lifetime mate who engages in those same addictive habits. Quite frankly two dead batteries will never start a car.

Each person's faults and weaknesses should appear as direct opposites in their spouse. This creates balance in the relationship. It is a well known fact that marriages born in nightclubs never seem to last too long. In any event a person should be able to quickly decide if a spouse is worth a little more investment or should they immediately sever the bonds of a failed marriage in order to cut the losses. In either case Jody is never too far away lurking in the backgrounds readily willing to volunteer to clean up the spill on isle three.

A prospective spouse should be able to bring as much if not more to the table. All worth should not be looked at in the form of tangible assets because sometimes an investment needs time to mature in order to receive the full face value, but in the words of the old farmer dressed in overalls along with tattered straw hat "you don't have to eat a whole hog to know if you're eating pork".

Whenever two choose to play the marriage game each participant should make their next move their best move. Continuous improvement processes apply to more than just the business world. To a marriage just learning to stand on its feet this can make the difference between life and death.

Believe it or not some people are better at digging themselves into a hole rather than digging out of one. It is a known fact that it takes as much effort to hustle backwards as it does to hustle forward, the only difference being which direction you choose to aim.

There should be an amendment to the current vows which are recited during a wedding - the new wording should contain the phrase "Do you take this man/woman to be your lawful husband/wife and promise to make it do what it do til death do you part?"

When You Smell Smoke But Can't Locate The Fire

*I*nfidelity has always played a pivotal part in marriages starting from the beginning of recorded documentation. What starts as an airtight union sealed by saying those magical words "I do" soon begin to exhibit signs of wear and tear in the form of small leaks usually undetectable at first glance. The relationship will continue to survive mainly on account of each person's intentional ignorance and willingness to adapt to subtle emotional changes that signify distance and detachment. The small unattentive leak soon evolves into a gaping hole big enough to drive a freightliner truck through.

The question is when and where did it all go wrong? Most acts of infidelity do not blossom overnight. These secondary attachments usually require months even years of performing acts of emotional servitude in order to prove trust and loyalty. Many come to the rational conclusion that before they risk marriage, home, and possibly children they must be assured the other person knows and appreciates all of the risk taken. This is why almost all of the people involved in infidelity choose to only desire a slice of the pie as opposed to eating the whole thing.

In the psychology field they have what is known as just noticeable difference (JND) which is a method of measuring the smallest amount of movement able to be detected by any human senses. The time to identify inconsistencies within a relationship is not after they have completely taken root but far in advance when the seeds of change interrupt the normal patterns of routines and familiar expectations.

A spouse adopting new habits which seem to appear from out of nowhere such as obtaining a sudden gym membership without previously showing the least amount of interest in body sculpting may be an early warning statement in itself. A desire to spend more time at the job in the form of coming in early or working late on a consistent basis in spite of there being no financial emergencies to validate such changes may have origins other than economic reasons.

It is a husband's or wife's responsibility to be aware of these changes no matter how discreet or unpretentious. A wife should know her husband's entire cologne collection by heart according to smell. This is important to know because one of the first things Jody does is to mark her/his territory by offering a new sense of smell designated to cause your spouse to think of them only. This is why it is always a good idea to go shopping with your spouse being actively involved with any suggestive purchases ranging from after shave cologne to matching panty and bra sets. While some may see this as overbearing there must also be some consideration for the statement "an ounce of prevention is worth a pound of cure".

Jody will never use aggressive tactics to infiltrate your marriage due to the fear of being detected before being able to adequately prepare bait for a deceptive trap. Instead Jody will employ the tricks of an old dog who is kept off the chain and told not to leave the yard. Everyday the dog while appearing to be innocent without any hint of malice or disobedience will playfully move another few inches towards the outer perimeter of the yard until one day without suspicion he will boldly not only leave the confines of the yard but even wander down the middle of the street ending up miles away from home. So many may wonder at what point did the dog decide to make his escape and the answer is clearly when the owner failed to no longer pay attention.

If you notice black clouds of charred ash emerging from your home along with the sharp smell of burning wood you would be a fool to say your house isn't on fire just because you failed to see any flames. By the same strategy

R Field Taylor

you shouldn't be so blind as to not notice your significant other slowly fading away into the background of infidelity.

There used to be a fairytale about a princess and a pea. The pea was hidden underneath a plush mattress and only a true princess would notice the discomfort when trying to sleep. Sure enough when the young lady of no known royalty was not able to sleep and upon searching for the cause of her irritation discovered the hidden pea beneath the mountain of mattresses it was immediately announced that the kingdom had found their new princess.

In a marriage when something doesn't feel right a person should follow their instincts. When you answer a phone and hear a sudden click. When you walk into a room and suddenly everyone stops talking. When you find the passenger seat in your spouse's vehicle adjusted to a different setting than for you. When your children continue to talk about your spouse's new cousin which you never met. When you're out with your spouse and someone calls you a name other than your own. And last but not least, when your spouse comes back home with more money than they left with (this is especially true for women).

We are reminded what the old blind woman stated to her cheating husband - "I might not can't see no more but I can sure smell bullshit".

Don't Let Everybody Make You Smile

⁕─────────⁙⊛⊛⊛⊙⊛⊛⊛⊙⊙─────────⁕

*I*n an older era people who were driving in a car on their way to some far away location sometimes would get lost along the way. The couple would then open the glove box and pull out a folded sheet of paper dotted with names, symbols, and numbers along the side intended to be as a reference points to show the location in order for the user to gauge how far away they were from reaching the desired destination. This entire process was called "reading a man".

A good map reader would be able to tell which route was the fastest or shortest and which route would lead them through a town enabling them to stop at a store if need be.

In a marriage sometimes a facial expression can be used as a road map to finding emotional destinations. For the new husband if Jody ever finds out how to make your wife smile he will use every tactic possible to keep her smiling. Sometimes he will show up from nowhere complete in hat with pointed spikes with bells attached while trying to balance on one leg. While this may look like harmless fun

Jody is a skilled entertainer who will hop and jingle his way right into your wife's underwear.

The female version Jody uses to make a man smile is a little more deceptive. Jody will wait for your husband to pull up at the gas station before she decides to get out of her car accidentally exposing as much area as possible between her thighs and waist due to a super ultra mini skirt and will make several circles around her vehicle in a feigned attempt to locate access to the gas cap. This act alone will cause your new husband to smile so bright it would seem as though he had just taken his teeth through the car wash.

After being saved from the near fatal dilemma of not knowing how to pump gas she will seize this moment to offer the famous slip of paper with her phone number and now Jody will have your husband paying for and pumping 93 octane at 2 AM in the morning even on holidays.

Guys don't think that you're the only one that can come home tired and stressed out from a long day at work because women go through the same challenges only in different formats. Your first instinct when either seeing your spouse off to work or greeting them when they arrive home should be how can I make her smile. But let's be honest, even for couples who have the best intentions there will be days when the best plan to maintain the peace will be to "stay the hell out of the way".

Jody knows that the eyes are a window to the soul but a smile is the front door to the bedroom. Don't let everybody make you smile.

Take Out Flood Insurance

adies, how many times have you seen a man full of modesty with an unassuming ego become an overnight sensation the moment you say your vows and place a ring on his finger?

The minute you capitalize on the unseen potential of your lifetime mate by dressing him in a new wardrobe, increasing his vocabulary, and upgrading his living conditions will cause hoes to flood your new husband faster than a broken toilet with the handle stuck in the flush position.

This was the same man in which no one even gave a second look before you agreed to marry him but now there exists an army of female Jodies waiting to catch you slipping. To protect yourself against the great multitudes of husband snatchers you must take out what we call "flood insurance".

Flood insurance is nothing more than insisting and requiring your name be attached to every minute object obtained after the marriage vows have been said. If a vehicle is purchased no matter what the cost make sure your name is on the title and insurance. You never know when you may need to bust a window or take a tag off in order to keep Jody

R Field Taylor

from riding away. You can't be arrested for damaging your own property.

Keep receipts for everything you give as a gift. The police will want to know if you actually own all of those clothes you set on fire in the driveway. Jody does not like having to replace an entire wardrobe.

Stay in good standing with all of the less fortunate people in your community. Pay for the wino's bottle of wine or give the homeless person some cigarette money. All of these acts are also part of flood insurance because these people are your eyes and ears on the street to let you know how many Jodys are circling your camp. They can even let you know what hotel your car is parked at even what room Jody lured your significant other to.

Remember the floodgates will open as soon as you say the words "I do".

Before You Earn Them You Have To Learn Them

When it comes down to the person you chose to walk down the isle with no one else should have more in depth knowledge of that person than you. You should be able to identify their farts from any other farts in a crowded room.

Nothing hurts more than learning some intimate detail about your spouse from a stranger you don't even know. You should already know what your wife and her 10th grade boyfriend did on prom night. You should know how many of your husband's baby mommas had abortions.

You should know how many STD's either of you have had in the past.

Just like a good weatherman can chart the path of an oncoming storm a wise and intelligent spouse should be able to predict the behavior of their significant other. You should know what food they will choose from the menu, what temperature they will adjust the thermostat to and even how long they will ride around with the gas light on.

Everyday after the wedding should be like sitting in the front row of class studying an anatomy chart with your spouse's picture attached. Not only should you be able to flawlessly forge their signature but also finish their sentences for them if need be.

All of these situations are characteristics of taking time to learn and know the person you're married to. The more time you invest in learning your spouse's thoughts, feelings and behaviors the more difficult it will be for Jody to insert his own propaganda and motives. A spouse should be seen as an investment offering a lifetime of residual benefits just as you would have detailed knowledge of your stock portfolio.

In certain situations Jody uses what you don't know about your spouse against you.

Take for example if Jody knows that your spouse's favorite white dog got ran over on Valentine's Day when she was only 16 years old he will go through the trouble of sending to her place of employment on any random February 14th an anonymous box of chocolates along with a box of holes on the side containing a beautiful little ball of white fur equipped with a collar saying "I'm back".

For any woman who does not know what to order her husband from the bar while he visits the restroom is in desperate need of a marriage tutor. She should know by heart he prefers Seagrams gin straight up on the rocks.

For Ladies Only - Learn The Best From a Prostitute

One of the most important lessons for the committed wife to remember is the same thing it took to get your husband it's gonna take the same thing to keep him.

The everyday wear and tear of being in a relationship can cause many couples to become emotionally distant. Many husbands will seek external remedies to bridge this void of sensual deficiency. Knowing they have neither the time or resources to devote to a full time alternative they seek out the temporary skilled services of a lady of the night. What makes these ladies an essential part of any stable marriage is that these women have learned to carry all of the burdens of husbands whose wives no longer feel it necessary to go the extra mile.

A prostitute can do wonders for a failing husband's self esteem, sometimes more than an entire room full of counselors with PhDs. They take the time to listen, sooth, and inspire men who no longer wait for wives to clock back in on their marriage duties. In many cases the wife has the prostitute to thank for her husband's enduring attitude of patience and acceptance. Without the few minutes of paid satisfaction from a dedicated whore the divorce rate would be on the incline along with domestic violence.

Ladies stop letting Jody give you a hand in your marriage. Find out what is missing or desired within your marriage relationship and fill in the blanks.

In many cases a majority of long term marriages could not have lasted but for the saving graces of a prostitute or side chick. In cases like these the MVP award should be presented from the trifling wife to the prostitute who gave more effort in the fourth quarter than the wife showed throughout the entire game. Maybe they should even name a pair of shoes for her "Air Ho".

All these considerations will not be publicly acknowledged even though they remain to be very factual.

The hidden message to be found within the texts is ladies don't allow yourselves to become slack on your wife's duties. In the event you develop a disregard for your "homework" just remember the clean up woman is always willing to work overtime.

The World Wide
Web Of Jody

*In a society as technologically advanced as our own it comes with no surprise that Jody has evolved into a highly computer literate weapon of mass destruction. There was an era when Jody had neither the time or patience to wait on dial-up connections to surf the available web for prey but now with the introduction of high speed internet along with computers which contain multiple processors Jody now has the capability to enter your bedroom and tell you the color of your spouse's underwear all with one click of the mouse.

The social media format operates off the addictive platform of self reassurance leaving many relationships, especially marriages, to become defined by how many likes or followers someone may have.

When people place their social inadequacies on public view for the world to observe, that becomes an instant beacon call to millions of Jodys male and female alike.

When a married woman decides to post a photo of

herself in revealing attire she is speaking a non verbal language which says "Tell me I look beautiful because I need to hear it." When Jody hears this subtle request for attention he is all too eager to fill her inbox with random comments such as "I know you are married but are you happily married?" Soon a correspondence will be created which will forever need to be kept in secret or deleted at the least. No matter how long the back and forth flirtations continue the end result is always the same with two people agreeing to meet up at some secluded location.

In most of these situations, Jody doesn't have to invest any huge sums of money to support his role play because the internet allows people to assume whatever character they choose to be. Today Jody is a lawyer, tomorrow he may be a talented CEO. Everything depends on which scenario will most benefit the agenda at hand.

Female Jodys have been tempting husbands over the years over the internet with thong pics and weave falling into the crevice of a partially exposed bosom. Some men even show their lustful interests in the forms of a variety of cash apps as to which they are readily able to offer up a resourceful lie to an inquiring wife if need be.

The only way to stop Jody from sabotaging your marriage through the internet is to follow the directions of a famous rap song entitled "No new friends". Remember, if Jody is able to steal, take, and carry away your spouse do not fault your local internet provider because they have no control over the power button which turns your computer on.

When It's Too Late To Cry

*S*ometimes the duration of a marriage a person may feel as though they've did everything the right way never giving their spouse a legitimate reason to find fault and still Jody ends up walking away with all the goods.

This will send some people into acts of depression or anger causing them to take a hard look at themselves in the mirror, oftentimes asking the question "What did I do wrong?"

The sad truth is that right doesn't always win and everyone is going to lose sometimes. So what do you do in a situation where you still have marriage papers on a man or woman that Jody has already taken away? You let them go. At first this may be the hardest thing to do because no one wants to stand idly by as a piece of their heart walks out of the door every night into the arms of someone else. The rule of thumb to remember is if they are strong enough to walk away you have to be strong enough to let them go. The reason for thinking this way is simple - Jody doesn't want anybody that nobody else wants.

The minute you stop showing interest in their

whereabouts or blowing up their phone every five minutes will cause some speculation between Jody and their new stolen prize.

To Jody the art of stealing is nothing more than one big adrenaline rush. Once the ill gotten prize appears to have lost its value Jody will return your loved one to your front door step faster than a fat man sitting down at a buffet.

In the unlikely event Jody does decide to keep your loved one then you have been given the authorization to have the biggest yard sale of the century - everything they left behind must go.

In the words of a great soul singer "one monkey don't stop no show".

Glossary

1) Buying a book: Usually when a man invests large amounts of time and resources into a woman who eventually ends up choosing someone else without warning.

2) Standing up in it: When a man shows excessive physical stamina during sexual intercourse.

3) Sugar Daddy: A man who takes on the financial responsibilities of a usually younger woman.

4) Old Man: Husband or boyfriend.

5) Old Lady: Wife or girlfriend.

6) Tricking: Trading sex for money.

7) Paid: Someone with large amounts of money.

8) Fall Back: Choosing not to become involved in drama.

9) Side chick/piece: A mistress.

10) Boy Toy: An older woman's younger sex partner.

11) Papers: Marriage certificate or license.

12) Creeping: Enacting elusive behavior while performing infidelity.

13) Kicked to the curb: When someone's spouse ends their relationship.

14) Downtown: (1) Oral sex (2) Police Department or Jail

15) Running game: The act of being deceptive and creating falsehoods.

16) Throwed: Mentally unstable.

17) Thick: A curvaceous female usually with wide hips and protruding buttocks along with large breasts.

18) Jody: Any male or female who knowingly has intimate affairs with someone else's spouse.

19) Clean up woman: A female who becomes quickly attached to a man who recently ended a relationship.

20) Crumb snatchers: Small children encountered during the dating process.

21) Snapper: A woman with exceptionally strong vaginal muscles.

22) Cooty Cat: Female vagina.

23) Brim: A man's dress hat.

24) Smoking: (1) An above average looking woman. (2) Someone involved in using crack cocaine.

25) Get a check: Being financially compensated for mental health reasons.

26) Hoopdy: An average vehicle for basic transportation.

27) Aunt Flo: A woman's menstrual period.

28) Take Back Man: Any repossession agent.

29) On the outs: A couple involved in separation or a serious disagreement.

30) Air Head: A very naive young woman.

31) Mama's Boy: A grown man still living at home with his mother.

32) Crib: Home or house used for physical residency.

33) Smell good: Any cologne or perfume.

34) Lame: Someone easily fooled or new to street life.

35) Down Low (DL): Secretive arrangements usually by two people who are in separate relationships.

36) Burning: A man or woman with a sexually transmitted disease.

37) Check In: Making a reassuring phone call or an appearance to an unsuspecting spouse.

38) Momo: A motel or hotel.

39) Fess Up: An admission of guilt.

40) Hoe Stroll: The act of being visibly seen attempting to entice someone.

Printed in the United States
by Baker & Taylor Publisher Services